I0446815

HOW TO OPEN A
HARDWARE STORE

A Comprehensive Guide to Starting, Running and
Growing Your Own Tools, Equipment and Supplies
Retailing Business

MORRIS WILLIS

Copyright Notice

This book is copyrighted in 2019-2022 by Dan & Elbert Associates.

All rights reserved.
Its content may not be copied or duplicated in part or whole by
any means without express prior agreement in writing

TABLE OF CONTENTS

Introduction

Welcome to a comprehensive guide designed for aspiring entrepreneurs venturing into the world of hardware stores. This book is your compass, your mentor, and your roadmap to navigate the intricate terrain of establishing, managing, and thriving in the hardware retail industry. Whether you're envisioning a neighborhood corner hardware shop or a modern hub for construction and DIY needs, this guide is tailored to help you navigate every step of the journey toward building a successful hardware store.

In these pages, you'll find a wealth of knowledge, insights, and practical advice distilled from years of collective experience in the hardware retail sector. From understanding the nuances of the hardware market to crafting a compelling business plan, sourcing inventory, fostering customer relationships, and leveraging technology, this book covers it all.

Launching a hardware store is more than just opening a shop; it's about creating a haven for home improvement enthusiasts, a go-to resource for contractors, and a trusted advisor for those embarking on DIY projects. It's about curating a diverse inventory, providing expert advice, and becoming an integral part of the community's growth and development.

Through these pages, we aim to ignite your passion, clarify your vision, and equip you with the tools and knowledge needed to build a thriving hardware store. Our goal is to inspire, guide, and support you on this entrepreneurial journey, ensuring that every step you take brings you closer to your dream of owning and operating a successful hardware store.

So, whether you're a seasoned professional in the industry or taking your first steps into the world of hardware retail, "Building Success" is here to be your companion, your mentor, and your guide as you embark on this exciting and rewarding venture of establishing your hardware store.

Why Start a Hardware Store?

Starting a hardware store offers a host of compelling reasons that make it an exciting venture. First off, these stores serve as crucial lifelines within neighborhoods, providing an extensive range of tools, materials, and know-how indispensable for construction, repairs, and do-it-yourself projects. By opening a hardware store, you're not just launching a business; you're becoming a dependable pillar of support for your local community, meeting essential needs and building trust among customers.

Moreover, hardware stores tap into a market with consistent demand. Regardless of economic fluctuations, people will always need tools, equipment, and supplies for their homes or projects, offering a steady customer base—a significant advantage for budding entrepreneurs.

Another appealing aspect is the diversity within the hardware retail industry. Whether you're inclined towards woodworking tools, sustainable materials, or specialized construction equipment, there's room to carve out a niche. This flexibility allows you to align your store with your passions, making the business financially viable and personally gratifying.

Furthermore, hardware stores can foster strong community connections. Beyond being a retail space, a well-managed hardware store can serve as a hub for workshops, demonstrations, and educational events. This engagement not only brings people together but also establishes your store as a knowledge hub, boosting its reputation and cultivating customer loyalty.

Ultimately, starting a hardware store presents an entrepreneurial canvas where innovation and personal touch flourish. You get to create a unique retail experience, curating products, delivering exceptional service, and crafting an inviting ambiance that sets your store apart from larger, impersonal chains.

In essence, opening a hardware store is more than just selling; it's about becoming an integral part of a community, meeting needs, offering expertise, and making a lasting impression while enjoying the rewards of entrepreneurship.

Is a Hardware Store Right for You?

Deciding whether a hardware store aligns with your aspirations and skills requires careful consideration of various factors. Firstly, a passion for DIY projects, construction, or home improvement can be a strong indicator of a good fit for running a hardware store. If you find joy in fixing things, helping others with projects, and have a genuine interest in tools and materials, this could be an ideal venture for you. Another crucial aspect is your entrepreneurial spirit and business acumen. Managing a hardware store involves handling inventory, finances, customer relations, and operational logistics. If you enjoy problem-solving, have a knack for organization, and possess a willingness to learn the intricacies of running a business, this endeavor might suit you well.

Understanding your local community and its needs is pivotal. A successful hardware store often caters to the specific requirements of its customer base. Being attuned to what your community lacks in terms of hardware supplies and services can give you a competitive edge and foster stronger connections with customers. Moreover, resilience and adaptability are essential traits. Running a hardware store, like any business, comes with its share of challenges—fluctuating market demands, competition, and unforeseen obstacles. Having the determination to weather these challenges and the flexibility to adapt to changing circumstances are key attributes for success.

Furthermore, consider your long-term goals and vision. Are you looking for a business that thrives on community engagement, where you can impart knowledge and create a sense of belonging? If building a legacy within your community and nurturing a business that serves as a trusted resource aligns with your aspirations, a hardware store might indeed be the right path for you.

Ultimately, evaluating your interests, skills, entrepreneurial drive, understanding of local needs, and long-term vision will help determine if a hardware store is a suitable venture that resonates with your goals and aspirations.

Chapter 1:
The Hardware Store Industry

The hardware store industry stands as a cornerstone of local communities, providing essential tools, materials, and expertise for construction, repairs, and do-it-yourself projects. It encompasses a diverse array of establishments, ranging from small, family-owned stores to large chain retailers. This industry's essence lies in catering to the needs of homeowners, contractors, craftsmen, and DIY enthusiasts alike.

At its core, the hardware store industry revolves around offering an extensive range of products and services, including hand and power tools, plumbing and electrical supplies, paint, building materials, gardening equipment, and household fixtures. These stores serve as hubs for essential items needed for maintenance, construction, or renovation projects, offering a one-stop destination for customers' hardware needs.

The success of hardware stores is deeply rooted in their ability to adapt to evolving customer demands and industry trends. Whether it's embracing eco-friendly products, introducing innovative tools, or leveraging digital technologies for customer engagement, the industry constantly evolves to meet the changing preferences and needs of consumers.

One defining aspect of the hardware store industry is its emphasis on personalized service and expert advice. Customers often seek guidance on product selection, usage, and project-specific recommendations. Hence, hardware stores distinguish themselves by fostering knowledgeable staff, often including professionals with expertise in various trades, who can offer valuable insights and assistance to customers.

The hardware industry's significance extends beyond mere commerce; these stores often serve as community hubs, providing a gathering place where locals exchange ideas, seek advice, and build relationships. Additionally, hardware stores frequently engage in community events, workshops, or educational programs, contributing to the neighborhood's social fabric.

Despite the rise of online retail and large-scale home improvement centers, the hardware store industry maintains its relevance through its personalized service, convenience, and local connections. These stores embody a sense of trust, reliability, and accessibility that resonates with customers seeking expertise and a sense of community in their hardware shopping experiences. As the industry continues to evolve, hardware stores remain an indispensable resource, empowering individuals to bring their projects and visions to life, one nail, tool, or paintbrush at a time.

Understanding the Hardware Market

Understanding the hardware market involves recognizing prevailing trends and identifying opportunities that drive the industry forward. This market, integral to construction, maintenance, and DIY projects, experiences constant evolution shaped by changing consumer preferences, technological advancements, and environmental consciousness.

One prominent trend within the hardware market is the growing emphasis on eco-friendly and sustainable products. Consumers increasingly seek environmentally conscious options, driving hardware stores to offer energy-efficient appliances, eco-friendly paints, and sustainable building materials. This trend aligns with a rising awareness of environmental impact, urging the industry to prioritize eco-friendly solutions.

Another significant trend revolves around technological integration. Hardware stores are leveraging technology to enhance customer experiences, streamline operations, and expand their reach. Online platforms, e-commerce capabilities, and mobile apps facilitate convenient purchasing options, while digital tools aid in inventory management and customer engagement. Smart home devices and innovative tools are also gaining popularity, reflecting the market's inclination toward tech-driven solutions.

Furthermore, the hardware market witnesses a shift in consumer behavior toward DIY projects and home improvement endeavors. The rise in home renovations, spurred by increased time spent at home and a desire for personalized living spaces, fuels demand for tools, materials, and expert advice. This trend creates opportunities for hardware stores to provide guidance, tutorials, and project-specific solutions to DIY enthusiasts and homeowners.

What Sets a Hardware Store Apart

What distinguishes a hardware store and sets it apart lies in its unique blend of offerings and customer-centric approach. Unlike generic retail outlets, hardware stores specialize in providing a comprehensive range of tools, materials, and expertise tailored to the needs of home improvement, construction, and maintenance.

Expertise and Knowledge: A standout feature of hardware stores is the knowledgeable staff who offer personalized advice and assistance. These stores often employ professionals with expertise in various trades, providing customers with invaluable guidance on product selection, usage, and project-specific recommendations.

Diverse Inventory: Hardware stores pride themselves on offering a diverse inventory of tools, building materials, plumbing and electrical supplies, paints, gardening equipment, and more. This extensive range allows customers to find specific items for their projects, distinguishing hardware stores as one-stop destinations for various needs.

Customer Service: Personalized service is a cornerstone of hardware stores. Staff members engage with customers, understanding their requirements, and providing tailored solutions. Whether it's offering recommendations, demonstrating product usage, or suggesting alternatives, hardware store staff ensure a positive and informative shopping experience.

Community Connection: Hardware stores often establish strong ties within their communities. They function as hubs where locals gather not only to shop but also to seek advice, exchange ideas, and attend workshops or events. This community connection fosters a sense of trust and reliability among customers.

Specialized Services: Many hardware stores offer additional services, such as key cutting, tool rental, equipment repair, and workshops. These value-added services enhance the overall customer experience, offering convenience and expertise beyond mere product sales.

Adaptability and Innovation: Hardware stores evolve by embracing technological advancements and incorporating innovative solutions. They integrate online platforms, e-commerce, and digital tools to expand their reach and cater to changing customer preferences while maintaining their traditional customer-centric approach.

Commitment to Quality: Hardware stores prioritize offering quality products and reliable brands, ensuring customer satisfaction and trust. By maintaining a commitment to quality, these stores establish themselves as dependable sources for durable and reliable tools and materials.

In essence, what sets a hardware store apart is its fusion of expertise, diverse inventory, personalized service, community connection, and commitment to quality. These elements combine to create an environment where customers not only find the tools and materials they need but also receive valuable guidance and support for their projects, fostering lasting relationships and loyalty within the community.

Passion and Vision: Essential Ingredients for Success

Passion and vision are the cornerstone for launching and nurturing a successful hardware store. Passion fuels the entrepreneurial spirit, driving the commitment to providing exceptional service and a diverse inventory of quality tools and materials. It's the deep enthusiasm for catering to the needs of DIY enthusiasts, contractors, and homeowners that propels the business forward, even during challenging times.

Vision, in the context of a hardware store, involves a clear roadmap outlining the store's objectives, target market, and service offerings. It's about envisioning the hardware store as a hub within the community, not merely as a retail space but as a knowledge center, offering expert advice and a diverse range of products. This vision encompasses the store's role in providing solutions, fostering customer relationships, and becoming a trusted resource for all things related to construction, maintenance, and DIY projects.

The fusion of passion and vision in launching a hardware store creates a vibrant atmosphere. It fuels the commitment to quality products, expert guidance, and exceptional customer service. This drive allows the store to cater to the community's needs, offering not just tools and materials but also expertise and a welcoming environment where customers feel valued and understood.

Moreover, this blend of passion and vision attracts like-minded individuals—enthusiastic staff who share the same dedication to serving customers and contributing positively to the community. It encourages teamwork and a shared commitment to the store's mission, fostering a culture of excellence and innovation.

Ultimately, in the realm of starting a hardware store, passion fuels the enthusiasm to embark on this journey, while vision provides the strategic direction and purpose necessary to establish a store that stands out as a trusted and indispensable resource within the community.

Chapter 2:
Market Research and Planning

In the world of business, the phrase "knowledge is power" couldn't be more accurate. Before embarking on the journey of starting your own hardware store, you need to arm yourself with a deep understanding of your market and a well-thought-out plan. This chapter is all about laying the groundwork for your hardware store venture, and it starts with four key components: Understanding Your Target Market, Choosing the Right Location, Competitive Analysis, and Creating a Business Plan.

Understanding Your Target Market

Understanding your target market is a pivotal step in successfully launching and running a hardware store. Firstly, conducting thorough market research helps identify the specific needs, preferences, and behaviors of your potential customer base. This involves analyzing demographics such as age, income level, location, and lifestyle to create a comprehensive profile of your target customers. Understanding the unique requirements of your local community is crucial. Consider factors like the prevalent types of projects undertaken, common repair and maintenance needs, and any specific trends or preferences within the area. This insight enables you to tailor your inventory, services, and marketing strategies to meet the demands of your specific market.

Analyzing the competition is essential. Studying existing hardware stores in the vicinity allows you to identify gaps in their offerings or areas where you can differentiate your store. Understanding what competitors are doing well and where they might be falling short helps in shaping your unique value proposition and positioning within the market. Also, engaging directly with your potential customer base through surveys, focus groups, or community events can provide invaluable insights. Listening to their feedback, understanding their pain points, and gauging their preferences helps in fine-tuning your product selection, pricing strategies, and customer service initiatives to better serve their needs.

A deep understanding of your target market lays the foundation for a hardware store that resonates with and meets the demands of your customers. It allows you to tailor your offerings, create a compelling shopping experience, and build lasting relationships within your community, fostering the success of your business.

Choosing the Right Location

Once you've gained a solid grasp of your hardware store's target market, the next crucial step is pinpointing the ideal location for your business. The location holds immense significance, and here's why it plays such a pivotal role:

Visibility and Accessibility: It's crucial for your store to be easily visible and accessible to your intended customers. Ideal locations often have high foot traffic and are close to residential areas, ensuring your store is easily found and convenient for shoppers.

Assessing Competition: Understanding the existing competition in your chosen area is vital. Are there established hardware stores nearby? What sets your store apart? Identifying market gaps or underserved customer segments can help your store stand out.

Matching Demographics: Ensure your chosen location aligns with the demographics and preferences of your target market. For instance, a hardware store in a family-centric area might prioritize affordability, while one near a health-conscious community may focus on organic products.

Zoning and Regulations: Local regulations and permits are critical considerations. These rules can impact your store's layout, operating hours, and product range. Compliance with local laws is essential for a successful business.

Financial Evaluation: Carefully analyze the financial aspects of your chosen location, including rent, utilities, and maintenance costs. Will this location yield a favorable return on investment? Conducting a thorough cost analysis is essential.

Consider collaborating with a commercial real estate agent specializing in retail spaces to navigate this decision effectively. These professionals can help identify locations aligned with your goals, negotiate lease terms, and ensure your chosen spot is an asset, not a liability.

Selecting the right location for your hardware store is foundational to its success. A well-chosen spot can drive traffic, differentiate you from competitors, and forge strong connections with your target market. By considering these factors and seeking expert guidance, you can make an informed decision that positions your store for success in the competitive retail market.

Competitive Analysis

Understanding your competition is crucial for carving out your niche in the hardware store market. A comprehensive competitive analysis is your compass, helping you navigate the complex terrain of this industry by identifying strengths, weaknesses, opportunities, and threats. Here's how to approach this vital process:

Start by compiling a comprehensive list of all existing hardware stores in your chosen area. However, don't limit your focus to just direct competitors. Consider nearby convenience stores, supermarkets, and even online hardware options that could potentially encroach on your market share. The broader your perspective, the more informed your analysis will be.

For each competitor on your list, conduct a SWOT analysis. This involves identifying their Strengths, such as unique product offerings, strong brand recognition, or a loyal customer base. Recognize their Weaknesses, which might include subpar customer service, limited product diversity, or outdated technology. Explore the Opportunities they might be missing, such as untapped market segments or emerging consumer trends. Lastly, assess the Threats they face, such as new entrants, economic downturns, or shifts in consumer preferences. This analysis will reveal valuable insights into the competitive landscape.

Now, it's time to define your hardware store's Unique Selling Proposition. What sets your establishment apart from the competition? Your USP could be a commitment to offering organic and locally sourced products, an unwavering dedication to providing exceptional customer service, or a promise to deliver unique in-store experiences that your rivals cannot match. Your USP is the beacon that attracts customers to your store.

Next, delve into the pricing strategies employed by your competitors. Are they positioned as premium stores, targeting high-end consumers, or do they cater to budget-conscious shoppers? Some may find a middle ground between these two extremes. Your pricing strategy should align seamlessly with both your target market and your identified USP. It's crucial to strike a balance between competitiveness and profitability. Whenever possible, research market share data for your chosen area. This data can provide valuable insights into the dominance of existing players in the market. Understanding who holds the largest piece of the pie and where there might be gaps or underserved segments can inform your strategic decisions. Remember that even if a competitor enjoys a substantial market share, there are often niches and segments they may not fully satisfy.

Conducting a thorough competitive analysis is like crafting a roadmap for your hardware store's success. It not only paints a clear picture of your market's landscape but also highlights potential growth opportunities and areas where your store can shine. By carefully considering the strengths, weaknesses, opportunities, and threats posed by your competitors, you can refine your business concept, create a winning strategy, and position your hardware store for long-term success in a fiercely competitive market.

Crafting a Comprehensive Business Plan

Now that you've gained a profound understanding of your target market, selected an optimal location, and gleaned insights into your competition, it's time to synthesize all this valuable information into a structured business plan. A business plan is your blueprint for steering your hardware store toward success. It encompasses several key components, each contributing to the overall framework of your vision:

Executive Summary: At the forefront of your business plan is the executive summary. This concise section encapsulates your business's essence, featuring your mission statement, overarching goals, and a summary of your financial forecasts.

Company Description: Dive deep into the intricacies of your hardware store in the company description section. Paint a vivid picture of your venture, elucidating your vision, the array of products you intend to offer, your unique selling propositions, and the profile of your target market.

Market Analysis: Summarize the insights gleaned from your thorough market research. Include pertinent details about your target market's demographics, the strategic choice of your location, and the competitive landscape you've uncovered.

Organization and Management: Provide an organizational blueprint. Who comprises your key team members, and what roles will they fulfill? Highlight relevant experience and qualifications that bolster your team's ability to execute your business strategy.

Products and Services: Outline an exhaustive list of the products and services that your hardware store will provide. Elaborate on any distinctive or specialty items in your inventory and elucidate your sourcing strategy.

Sales and Marketing: Articulate your sales and marketing strategies in detail. How will you entice and retain customers? Detail your advertising campaigns, promotional tactics, and the channels you'll employ to reach your audience effectively.

Funding Request: If you're seeking external financing, elucidate your funding needs. Specify precisely how you intend to allocate these funds and outline the terms you're seeking from potential investors or lenders.

Financial Projections: Underpin your plan with meticulous financial projections. Include comprehensive income statements, balance sheets, and cash flow statements that extend at least three to five years into the future. These projections offer a tangible picture of your financial trajectory.

Appendix: Finally, compile any supplemental documents that buttress your business plan. This might encompass market research data, resumes showcasing the expertise of key team members, and essential supplier agreements.

Remember that your business plan isn't a static document; it should evolve alongside your business. It serves as a dynamic tool for strategizing, decision-making, and effectively conveying your vision to potential investors and stakeholders. With a robust business plan in hand, you'll be better equipped to navigate the dynamic hardware store landscape and steer your venture toward long-term success.

Chapter 3:
Legal and Regulatory Considerations

Starting and operating a hardware store involves navigating a complex web of legal and regulatory requirements. Understanding and complying with these rules is essential to ensure the smooth and legal operation of your business. In this chapter, we'll explore the key legal and regulatory considerations for your hardware store, including choosing the right business structure, obtaining permits and licenses, adhering to health and safety regulations, and managing taxation.

Choosing a Business Structure

One of the first decisions you'll need to make when starting your hardware store is choosing the right business structure. The structure you select will have implications for your personal liability, taxation, and how you can raise capital. Here are some common business structures to consider:

Sole Proprietorship: This is the simplest and most common form of business ownership. As a sole proprietor, you have complete control over your hardware store, but you are personally responsible for all business debts and liabilities. Your business income and expenses are reported on your personal tax return.

Partnership: If you plan to start your hardware store with one or more partners, a partnership structure may be suitable. Partnerships can be general partnerships (where partners share equally in profits and liabilities) or limited partnerships (where some partners have limited liability). Like sole proprietors, partners report their share of business income and expenses on their personal tax returns.

Limited Liability Company (LLC): An LLC provides a level of personal liability protection for its owners (called members). Members are typically not personally responsible for the company's debts and liabilities. LLCs offer flexibility in management and taxation, as they can be taxed as a sole proprietorship, partnership, or corporation.

Corporation: A corporation is a separate legal entity from its owners (shareholders). This structure offers the most significant personal liability protection, as shareholders are generally not personally liable for the company's debts. Corporations also have the advantage of attracting outside investors by issuing shares of stock. However, corporations have more complex tax and regulatory requirements.

Cooperative (Co-op): A cooperative is owned and operated by its members, who share in the decision-making and profits. Hardware store cooperatives are often formed by a group of individuals with a shared interest. Co-ops have unique governance structures and may be organized as LLCs, corporations, or other legal entities.

Choosing the right business structure is a critical decision that should align with your long-term goals and financial considerations. Consult with legal and financial advisors to assess the best option for your hardware store.

Permits and Licenses

Running a hardware store requires various permits and licenses to comply with local, state, and federal regulations. These licenses and permits demonstrate that your store meets specific health, safety, and operational standards. Here's an overview of the essential permits and licenses you may need:

Business License: Most cities or municipalities require businesses to obtain a general business license. This license allows you to operate legally within a specific jurisdiction. The requirements and fees for business licenses vary by location.

Sales Tax Permit: Also known as a sales tax license or resale permit, this allows your hardware store to collect sales tax from customers on behalf of the state. It's necessary for selling taxable goods and services.

Building Permits: If you're constructing or renovating your store space, building permits are essential. They ensure that your construction plans comply with local building codes, safety standards, and zoning regulations.

Signage Permits: These permits are needed for any external signage you plan to install for your store. Regulations regarding size, placement, and type of signage vary by location and must be adhered to.

Occupational Permits: Depending on your locality, you might need specific occupational permits or licenses related to the hardware retail industry. These could include licenses for handling hazardous materials, operating power tools, or providing certain services.

Health and Safety Permits: If your store offers services like key cutting or tool repair, you might need health and safety permits to ensure compliance with regulations related to these services.

It's essential to research and understand the specific permits and licenses required in your area. Contact your local government offices or regulatory authorities to obtain detailed information about the necessary permits and the application process. Non-compliance with these regulations can result in fines, legal issues, or even the closure of your business. Therefore, ensuring that you have all the required permits and licenses in place before opening your hardware store is crucial for its legal and operational integrity.

Taxation

Understanding the taxation aspects of your hardware store is crucial for managing your finances and complying with tax laws. Here are key tax considerations:

Sales Tax: Most states and local jurisdictions impose sales tax on the sale of tangible goods. You are responsible for collecting and remitting sales tax to the appropriate taxing authorities. It's essential to understand the specific tax rates and exemptions that apply to hardware items in your area.

Income Tax: Your hardware store's income is subject to federal and state income taxes. The business structure you choose will determine how your income is taxed. Sole proprietors report business income on their personal tax returns, while corporations have separate tax obligations.

Employee Payroll Taxes: If you have employees, you must withhold and remit payroll taxes, including federal income tax, Social Security tax, and Medicare tax. Employers also pay a portion of these taxes.

Property Tax: Real property, such as the land and buildings housing your hardware store, is subject to property tax. The amount of property tax you pay depends on the assessed value of your property and local tax rates.

Licensing and Permit Fees: Some licenses and permits may have associated fees that must be paid on a regular basis.

Use Tax: If your state imposes a use tax, you may be required to pay it on items purchased out of state for use in your business.

Business Deductions: Take advantage of tax deductions available to hardware stores. These may include deductions for business expenses such as rent, utilities, advertising, and employee salaries.

Accounting and Recordkeeping: Maintain accurate financial records and accounting practices to facilitate tax compliance and reporting. Consider working with a certified public accountant (CPA) or tax professional to ensure accuracy.

Tax Credits and Incentives: Research if there are any tax credits or incentives available for hardware stores in your region. Some areas offer incentives for businesses that promote healthy eating or invest in energy-efficient equipment.

Filing Deadlines: Familiarize yourself with tax filing deadlines and make sure you submit all required tax forms and payments on time to avoid penalties and interest.

Navigating the complexities of taxation can be challenging, so it's advisable to consult with a tax professional or CPA with experience in the retail and hardware industry. They can help you maximize deductions, plan for tax liabilities, and ensure compliance with tax laws.

The legal and regulatory considerations for a hardware store are multifaceted and demand meticulous attention. Choosing the right business structure, obtaining the necessary permits and licenses, adhering to health and safety regulations, and managing taxation are fundamental aspects of running a successful and legally compliant hardware store. By investing the time and effort to understand and meet these requirements, you lay a solid foundation for the growth and longevity of your business.

Chapter 4:
Financing Your Hardware Store

Financing is a critical aspect of launching and sustaining a successful hardware store. In this chapter, we will explore the key elements of financing your hardware store, including estimating startup costs, securing funding from various sources, and managing your finances effectively.

Estimating Startup Costs

Before you open your hardware store's doors, it's essential to determine the initial investment required to get your business off the ground. Estimating startup costs accurately will help you secure the necessary funding and avoid financial pitfalls. Here are some primary components to consider when calculating your startup expenses:

Location Costs: The cost of securing and preparing your store location, including lease or purchase costs, renovations, and any necessary permits.

Equipment and Fixtures: Expenses related to purchasing or leasing equipment such as refrigerators, freezers, shelving, cash registers, and point-of-sale (POS) systems.

Inventory: The initial inventory of products you'll stock in your store. This can vary depending on the size and focus of your hardware store.

Licenses and Permits: Fees associated with obtaining the required licenses and permits, which can include health permits, business licenses, and signage permits.

Legal and Professional Fees: Costs for legal assistance, such as hiring an attorney to help with business structure and contract reviews, as well as fees for consultants and advisors.

Marketing and Advertising: Funds allocated for marketing strategies and advertising campaigns to promote your store's opening and attract customers.

Employee Costs: Budget for hiring and training staff during the startup phase. Include salaries, benefits, and any recruitment expenses.

Utilities and Rent: Projections for monthly rent or lease payments, utility bills, and security deposits.

Insurance: Costs associated with business insurance, including liability, property, and workers' compensation insurance.

Technology and Software: Expenses for computer systems, software, and POS systems to manage sales and inventory.

Working Capital: Funds reserved for initial operational expenses, such as purchasing additional inventory, covering payroll, and managing cash flow until the store becomes profitable.

Contingency Fund: A buffer for unexpected expenses or setbacks that may arise during the startup phase.

Marketing and Grand Opening Costs: Budget for promotional events and marketing efforts surrounding your store's grand opening.

Miscellaneous Expenses: Allow for miscellaneous costs, such as office supplies, signage, and initial marketing materials.

It's crucial to create a detailed financial plan that outlines these costs and provides a realistic estimate of your startup expenses. Be prepared to revisit and adjust your budget as you gather more information and refine your business plan.

Securing Funding

Once you have a clear understanding of your startup costs, the next step is to secure the necessary funding. Financing your hardware store may require a combination of personal savings, loans, investments, and grants. Here are some common sources of funding:

Personal Savings: Using your own savings to finance your hardware store is a common and straightforward approach. It allows you to maintain full control of your business and eliminates the need to pay interest on loans.

Family and Friends: Some entrepreneurs turn to family members or close friends for financial support. While this can be an accessible source of funding, it's crucial to formalize any agreements in writing to avoid misunderstandings.

Small Business Loans: Banks and credit unions offer various types of small business loans, including term loans, lines of credit, and equipment financing. These loans often require a solid business plan and collateral.

SBA Loans: The U.S. Small Business Administration (SBA) provides loan programs to support small businesses. SBA loans typically have favorable terms and lower interest rates, but they also involve a rigorous application process.

Investors: Seek investors who are willing to provide capital in exchange for equity or a share of the profits. Angel investors, venture capitalists, and private equity firms are potential sources of investment.

Crowdfunding: Crowdfunding platforms, such as Kickstarter and Indiegogo, allow you to raise funds from a large number of people online. This method is particularly effective if you have a unique and compelling business concept.

Grants: Some government agencies, non-profit organizations, and foundations offer grants to support small businesses, especially those focused on community development or sustainable practices.

Supplier Financing: Negotiate favorable payment terms with your suppliers. Some suppliers may offer extended payment periods, allowing you to manage cash flow more effectively.

Franchise Opportunities: If you're considering opening a franchise hardware store, the franchisor may provide financing options or assistance with securing loans.

Online Lenders: Online lending platforms offer various financing options, including short-term loans, business lines of credit, and invoice financing. These options may be more accessible for newer businesses.

Government Programs: Research local and state government programs that provide financial assistance, grants, or tax incentives to small businesses, especially those creating jobs or contributing to the local economy.

Alternative Funding: Explore alternative funding sources, such as merchant cash advances, factoring, or peer-to-peer lending. These options may be suitable for businesses with unique financing needs.

To secure funding successfully, you'll need to prepare a compelling business plan that demonstrates the viability and profitability of your hardware store. Lenders and investors want to see that you have a clear vision, a solid market strategy, and a realistic financial forecast. Be prepared to provide financial statements, cash flow projections, and any collateral if required.

Managing Finances

Managing the finances of a catering business is crucial for its long-term success. It involves various essential practices to ensure effective financial control. Firstly, keeping accurate records of all financial transactions is key. This includes tracking income from events and expenses related to ingredients, equipment, staff wages, and other operational costs. Using reliable accounting software helps in keeping these records organized and precise.

Monitoring cash flow is another critical aspect. Catering businesses often experience fluctuations in income based on event bookings and seasonal demands. Therefore, keeping a close eye on money coming in and going out helps ensure there's enough cash to cover essential expenses, buy necessary supplies, pay employees, and manage unexpected costs. Creating cash flow projections assists in planning ahead for financial needs.

Crafting a detailed budget is essential. It should outline expected revenues and breakdown expenses, encompassing everything from ingredients and equipment to marketing and staffing costs. Regularly comparing the actual financial performance with the budget allows for adjustments to maintain financial stability.

Efficiently managing inventory is important too. Balancing inventory levels to meet demand without unnecessary stockpiling is crucial for financial health. Keeping an eye on stock levels and turnover rates helps in managing inventory effectively, minimizing waste, and maximizing profits.

Cost control is another significant aspect. Analyzing expenses and finding ways to reduce costs without compromising quality is vital. Negotiating better terms with suppliers, exploring bulk purchasing options, and optimizing staffing are effective strategies to manage costs.

Lastly, ensuring compliance with tax obligations, maintaining proper financial records, and regularly reviewing financial performance through reports like income statements and balance sheets are essential practices. Seeking advice from accountants or financial advisors specializing in the catering industry can offer valuable insights for making informed financial decisions and improving profitability. Managing finances in a catering business requires diligence and proactive strategies to ensure financial stability and support sustainable growth.

Chapter 5:
Store Design and Layout

The design and layout of your hardware store play a pivotal role in shaping the customer experience, optimizing efficiency, and driving sales. In this chapter, we will delve into the critical aspects of store design and layout, including store layout considerations, shelving and merchandising strategies, equipment and fixtures, and interior design.

Store Layout Considerations

Designing an effective store layout necessitates careful planning to create a shopping environment that caters to your customers' needs while optimizing sales. Here are several key store layout considerations:

Customer Flow: Plan a layout that guides customers smoothly through the store. Consider placing frequently purchased items towards the entrance to attract attention and encourage exploration deeper into the store. Create clear pathways that make it easy for customers to navigate and find what they need.

Product Placement: Organize products logically based on categories and usage frequency. Group related items together, such as plumbing supplies or electrical tools, to facilitate easy shopping and enhance the customer experience. Highlight popular or seasonal items prominently.

Aisles and Shelving: Optimize aisle width for easy movement and accommodate carts or trolleys. Adjustable shelving allows flexibility to accommodate various product sizes. Ensure shelves are well-stocked, neatly organized, and labeled clearly for effortless browsing.

Checkout Area: Strategically position checkout counters to minimize wait times and create a seamless checkout process. Consider additional displays near the checkout area for last-minute purchases or impulse buys.

Accessibility: Ensure the store layout is accessible to all customers, including those with disabilities. Maintain clear pathways, provide ramps or elevators where necessary, and ensure that product displays are reachable for all customers.

Safety and Comfort: Prioritize safety by keeping aisles clear of obstructions, ensuring proper lighting, and maintaining a clean and hazard-free environment. Incorporate comfortable waiting areas for customers and seating for those in need of assistance or consultation.

Flexibility and Adaptability: Design the layout with flexibility in mind to accommodate changes in inventory, seasonal displays, or promotional setups. This adaptability allows for easy modifications to meet evolving customer needs and store requirements.

Testing and Demonstration Areas: Consider allocating space for customers to test tools or equipment. Providing demonstration areas enhances customer engagement and allows for hands-on experience, influencing purchase decisions.

Employee Accessibility: Design employee workstations strategically to facilitate efficient restocking, inventory management, and customer assistance. Ensure staff areas are easily accessible but not obstructive to customer flow.

By considering these store layout considerations, you can create an inviting, efficient, and customer-friendly environment that maximizes sales potential and enhances the overall shopping experience at your hardware store.

Shelving and Merchandising

Effective shelving and merchandising are fundamental elements in the art of presenting products attractively, optimizing space, and ultimately driving sales. To achieve these goals, consider implementing the following strategies:

Shelving Types: Choose shelving that suits the variety of products in your store. Adjustable shelves allow flexibility for different-sized items, while specialized shelving, like pegboards or gridwall systems, cater to specific merchandise, such as tools or accessories.

Product Organization: Arrange products logically and aesthetically. Group similar items together, utilizing categories or project themes to guide customers. Use clear signage and labels for easy navigation and identification of products.

Planogram Implementation: Develop a planogram—a visual representation of how products are displayed on shelves—to optimize space and improve sales. It helps determine where products should be placed for maximum visibility and appeal.

Eye-Level Placement: Place high-demand or premium items at eye level to capture customer attention. This prime shelf space tends to attract more attention and encourages purchases.

Cross-Merchandising: Pair complementary items together to encourage multiple purchases. For example, display paintbrushes next to paint cans or lightbulbs near fixtures. Cross-merchandising encourages customers to buy related products in one shopping trip.

Seasonal Displays: Utilize shelving and displays to highlight seasonal or promotional items. Rotate merchandise based on seasons or upcoming holidays to capitalize on customer needs and preferences.

Visual Merchandising: Use visual techniques like color coordination, attractive displays, and well-organized shelves to create an appealing shopping environment. Incorporate informative signage or demo areas to educate customers about products.

Inventory Management: Regularly restock shelves to ensure products are readily available and well-presented. Implement inventory management systems to track stock levels and avoid out-of-stock situations.

Safety Measures: Ensure shelving units are sturdy, well-maintained, and meet safety standards to prevent accidents or injuries. Avoid overcrowding shelves to maintain a safe shopping environment.

Employee Training: Train staff on effective merchandising techniques and the importance of maintaining a well-organized and visually appealing store. Empower them to assist customers in finding products and providing product knowledge.

Effective shelving and merchandising strategies not only enhance the shopping experience but also contribute to increased sales, customer satisfaction, and a positive in-store atmosphere for your hardware store.

Equipment and Fixtures

When setting up a hardware store, acquiring the right equipment and fixtures is crucial for operational efficiency and creating an inviting shopping environment. Consider the following essential items:

Shelving and Racking: Invest in sturdy and versatile shelving units to display a variety of products. Adjustable shelves allow flexibility in accommodating different-sized items and adjusting layouts as needed. Racking systems are ideal for storing larger, bulkier items like lumber or pipes.

Display Fixtures: Use various display fixtures such as pegboards, gridwall systems, or slatwall panels to showcase tools, accessories, or smaller items. These fixtures offer flexibility in arranging merchandise and maximizing space.

Point-of-Sale (POS) System: Implement a reliable POS system to manage sales, track inventory, and process transactions efficiently. Choose a system that suits the scale and needs of your hardware store, integrating features like inventory management and reporting tools.

Storage Solutions: Invest in storage solutions like bins, drawers, or cabinets to organize smaller hardware items, fasteners, or parts. Clear storage containers with labels facilitate easy identification and access to inventory.

Cash Register and Checkout Equipment: Set up robust and user-friendly cash registers or POS terminals at checkout counters. Equip these areas with barcode scanners, receipt printers, and card payment terminals for smooth transactions.

Security Equipment: Install security systems like cameras, alarms, and theft deterrents to safeguard your store and inventory.

Adequate lighting and visible security measures can deter potential theft.

Material Handling Equipment: Consider equipment like hand trucks, forklifts, or carts to handle heavy or bulky items. These aids streamline stocking, organizing, and moving merchandise around the store.

Signage and Display Materials: Utilize signage, banners, and display materials for product promotion, pricing, or highlighting special offers. Clear and informative signage guides customers and enhances their shopping experience.

Workstations and Tools: Equip workstations with necessary tools for providing customer service, cutting materials, or assisting with projects. Ensure employees have access to tools like saws, drills, or measuring equipment for store operations.

Lighting and Fixtures: Install adequate lighting fixtures to ensure a well-lit and inviting atmosphere. Use a combination of ambient, task, and accent lighting to highlight merchandise and create a comfortable shopping environment.

Choosing durable, functional, and visually appealing equipment and fixtures is integral to the success of your hardware store. Tailor these items to suit your store layout, customer needs, and operational requirements for a well-equipped and customer-friendly establishment.

Interior Design

Designing the interior of a hardware store is like crafting an experience for shoppers, where every element contributes to their comfort and convenience. The layout is a critical aspect, ensuring that aisles, displays, and checkouts are strategically placed for easy navigation and efficient operations.

Lighting plays a significant role, creating a welcoming atmosphere and showcasing products effectively. The right balance of natural and artificial light contributes not only to visibility but also to the overall sense of cleanliness and safety in the store.

Colors subtly influence the mood of the store. Warm and inviting tones create a comfortable ambiance, while strategic color use can highlight promotions or specific sections. Branding elements and signage add to the visual appeal and help customers easily recognize and navigate through the store.

Product displays are crucial for both aesthetics and sales. Well-organized shelves, attractive endcap displays, and eye-catching promotions draw attention to products and encourage spontaneous purchases. Grouping similar items together enhances the convenience of the shopping experience.

Checkout counters are central points of customer interaction. Designing these areas for efficiency and customer satisfaction, with features like express lanes and well-organized impulse-buy sections, contributes to a positive overall impression.

Incorporating technology adds a modern touch to hardware store design. Digital signage, interactive displays, and mobile checkout options not only enhance the store's appearance but also engage customers and make their shopping experience more convenient.

Safety and accessibility are paramount considerations in hardware store interior design. Ensuring adequate space for wheelchair users, clear emergency exits, and a well-designed customer service area contribute to an inclusive and secure shopping environment.

In essence, the interior design of a hardware store is a blend of functionality and aesthetics, aimed at creating a pleasant and efficient shopping experience. From the layout to lighting, colors, displays, and technology, each element plays a role in shaping the atmosphere and influencing customer behavior for the success of the store.

The design and layout of your hardware store are critical elements that influence customer experience, operational efficiency, and sales performance. By carefully considering store layout, shelving and merchandising strategies, equipment and fixtures, and interior design, you can create a shopping environment that attracts customers, encourages sales, and sets your hardware store apart from the competition.

Chapter 6:
Product Selection and Suppliers

The success of your hardware store heavily relies on the products you offer and the relationships you build with suppliers. In this chapter, we will delve into the critical aspects of product selection and suppliers, including building relationships with suppliers, managing inventory effectively, implementing pricing strategies, and considering private label products as part of your inventory.

Product Selection

P roduct selection for a hardware store requires a careful and strategic approach to cater to the diverse needs of customers. A well-curated inventory is essential to meet the demands of both professionals and DIY enthusiasts. The process begins with thorough market research to understand current trends, emerging technologies, and the specific needs of the local community. This insight helps in identifying the most sought-after tools, equipment, and materials that customers are likely to seek.

The selection process involves considering a wide range of categories, including hand and power tools, building materials, plumbing and electrical supplies, paints, hardware accessories, and safety equipment. Offering a comprehensive assortment within each category ensures that customers find a variety of choices to suit their requirements, whether it's a professional contractor looking for specialized tools or a homeowner tackling a weekend DIY project.

Striking the right balance between well-known, trusted brands and more affordable yet reliable alternatives is crucial. High-quality products from reputable brands build customer trust, while providing budget-friendly options expands accessibility and caters to a wider customer base. Additionally, regularly updating the inventory to include innovative tools or eco-friendly alternatives reflects the store's commitment to staying current with industry advancements and meeting evolving consumer preferences.

Furthermore, understanding the seasonal demands and regional preferences is pivotal. For instance, stocking up on landscaping and gardening tools in the spring or snow removal equipment in colder regions during winter enhances customer satisfaction and drives sales. Regularly reviewing and refining the product selection based on sales data, customer feedback, and market trends ensures the hardware store remains responsive to changing customer needs and preferences. Ultimately, a well-thought-out product selection not only meets immediate customer demands but also establishes the hardware store as a reliable destination for all construction, repair, and DIY needs.

Building Relationships with Suppliers

Building strong and lasting relationships with suppliers is a crucial aspect of running a successful hardware store. These partnerships not only ensure a steady supply of products but also offer various benefits that can positively impact your business.

Firstly, effective communication is the foundation of any strong supplier relationship. Open and transparent lines of communication foster trust and understanding between you and your suppliers. Regularly discussing your needs, concerns, and expectations can lead to better collaboration and problem-solving when issues arise.

Another key element in building supplier relationships is reliability. Consistently meeting payment deadlines and honoring agreements demonstrates your commitment and reliability as a business partner. This reliability can lead to better terms, such as discounts, extended credit, or priority access to high-demand products.

Mutual respect is essential. Treating your suppliers with respect and professionalism, just as you expect from them, creates a positive working environment. This can lead to better customer service, faster response times, and a willingness to go the extra mile to support your store. Building trust takes time and effort. One way to foster trust is by sharing your business plans and goals with your suppliers. When suppliers understand your vision, they can tailor their offerings and support to align with your objectives.

Collaboration is also key in supplier relationships. Engaging in joint initiatives, such as marketing campaigns or product development, can be mutually beneficial. This not only strengthens the bond but can also lead to innovative solutions and increased sales.

Regularly reviewing and evaluating your supplier relationships is vital. Assess the quality of products, delivery timelines, and the overall value they bring to your business. If issues arise, address them promptly and constructively, seeking solutions that benefit both parties.

Building relationships with suppliers is not just about transactions; it's about creating partnerships that benefit both your hardware store and your suppliers. Open communication, reliability, mutual respect, trust, collaboration, and regular evaluation are the pillars of successful supplier relationships. Investing time and effort in nurturing these relationships can contribute significantly to your store's success and sustainability.

Managing Inventory

Having secured suppliers and goods starts coming in, you would have to manage your inventories. Effective inventory management involves several key components that work together to ensure you have the right products in the right quantities at the right times.

One fundamental aspect of inventory management is accurate tracking. This entails keeping detailed records of your inventory levels, product turnover rates, and reorder points. Utilizing modern inventory management software can streamline this process, providing real-time insights into your stock levels and helping you make informed decisions.

Strategic purchasing is another crucial element. It involves ordering products in quantities that align with your store's demand patterns and sales trends. Analyzing historical sales data can help you forecast future demand and avoid overstocking or understocking items, which can tie up capital or result in missed sales opportunities.

Categorizing your inventory into different classifications can also be beneficial. Items can be categorized as fast-moving, slow-moving, or non-moving, allowing you to allocate resources more effectively. Fast-moving items may require frequent restocking, while slow-moving or non-moving items may warrant different management strategies, such as promotions or clearance sales.

Implementing inventory control measures can help prevent issues like theft, spoilage, or obsolescence. This can involve using security systems, monitoring expiration dates, and regularly inspecting inventory for damage or discrepancies.

Regularly conducting physical inventory counts is essential for accuracy. Periodic audits ensure that your recorded inventory levels align with the actual quantities on your shelves and in your storage areas. It's a time-consuming process, but the benefits in terms of accurate record-keeping and minimizing discrepancies are invaluable.

Effective inventory management also involves developing relationships with your suppliers. Establishing clear communication channels, negotiating favorable terms, and collaborating on supply chain efficiencies can help ensure a reliable and cost-effective flow of products into your store.

Finally, embracing technology can significantly enhance your inventory management efforts. Utilizing inventory management software, barcode scanning systems, and automated reorder triggers can streamline processes, reduce errors, and improve overall efficiency. Managing inventory in a hardware store requires a multifaceted approach that encompasses accurate tracking, strategic purchasing, categorization, control measures, physical counts, supplier relationships, and the integration of technology. By effectively managing your inventory, you can optimize your store's operations, maximize profitability, and provide a satisfying shopping experience for your customers.

Pricing Strategies

Pricing strategies serve as essential tools for boosting product sales and optimizing profits within a hardware store. Recognizing the significance of these strategies is paramount as they profoundly impact customer behavior, subsequently influencing the store's profitability and overall revenue. Finding the right equilibrium between competitive pricing, which attracts customers, and sustaining profit margins is vital for the long-term success of the business. This delicate balance ensures both customer satisfaction and financial stability, fostering sustained growth and prosperity for the hardware store.

Here's how we can adapt that information for a hardware store:

Dynamic Pricing:

Dynamic pricing is a powerful tool for your hardware store, allowing you to adjust prices in real time based on various factors like demand, competition, and seasonal trends. This strategy enables you to optimize prices according to market conditions, ensuring competitiveness and maximizing value capture. Think of your favorite ride-sharing app — it's a prime example of how dynamic pricing responds to changing demand. Implementing this approach can help your hardware store stay agile and align prices with market dynamics, enhancing competitiveness and meeting customer demand effectively.

Value-Based Pricing
One common pricing strategy is value-based pricing, where the store adds a markup to the cost of goods to determine the selling price. This approach ensures that the store covers its expenses and generates a profit. However, it may not consider market demand or competition, potentially leading to overpricing or underpricing.

Competitive pricing is another widely used strategy. In this approach, hardware stores set their prices in line with or slightly below the prices offered by their competitors. This strategy aims to attract price-conscious shoppers and maintain competitiveness in the market. Regular price monitoring and adjustments are essential to stay competitive.

Dynamic pricing is gaining traction, particularly in online hardware retail. It involves adjusting prices based on real-time data, such as demand, inventory levels, and competitor pricing. Dynamic pricing allows stores to maximize revenue by charging higher prices during peak demand periods and offering discounts during slower times.

Promotional pricing is a valuable tool to drive sales and customer loyalty. It includes strategies like discounts, buy-one-get-one-free (BOGO) offers, and loyalty programs. These promotions attract shoppers looking for deals and can boost sales for specific products or categories.

Psychological pricing tactics leverage consumer psychology to influence purchasing decisions. These tactics include using pricing endings like "$0.99" instead of rounding to the nearest dollar or emphasizing savings by showing a "discounted" price alongside the regular price. Such tactics create a perception of value and can lead to increased sales.

Price elasticity is an essential concept in pricing strategy. It measures how sensitive customer demand is to changes in price. Products with inelastic demand, such as essential tools, can tolerate price increases without significant decreases in sales. However, products with elastic demand, like luxury items, are more sensitive to price changes.

Strategic pricing should consider the overall store positioning and target market. A store focusing on premium or organic products may employ higher pricing to align with its brand image, while a store catering to budget-conscious shoppers may adopt a more aggressive pricing strategy.

Penetration Pricing is a strategic approach utilized by hardware stores when entering a new market. In this method, aggressive initial pricing is set for the products on offer. By presenting introductory lower prices, the store aims to entice price-sensitive buyers and establish a customer base seeking better value in products. However, it's essential to view this pricing strategy from a long-term perspective, ensuring profitability and sustainability over time.

In your hardware store, setting prices is an ongoing process that demands constant attention, analysis, and adjustment. By employing test and learn methodologies, you can experiment with diverse pricing strategies, assess their impact, and refine your approach accordingly. This iterative approach allows you to continuously improve and adapt your pricing strategies to the ever-changing market dynamics.

It's crucial to stay abreast of industry trends and keep a keen eye on competitor activities. Regularly monitoring your competitors' pricing strategies, promotional campaigns, and market trends offers valuable insights and opportunities for adjusting your pricing strategy. This competitive intelligence empowers you to make informed pricing decisions, ensuring your hardware store maintains a competitive edge in the market.

Utilizing effective pricing strategies like dynamic pricing, value-based pricing, psychological pricing, and penetration pricing can work wonders. These strategies help attract customers, add value to your offerings, and ultimately boost your profitability. It's crucial to tap into data-driven insights, keep an eye on market trends, and stay updated with industry shifts to consistently refine your pricing decisions.

Pricing isn't a one-time fix; it's an ongoing journey that demands flexibility and a bit of experimentation. By adopting these retail pricing strategies, hardware stores can adapt better to customer demands and the ever-changing market conditions. It's all about positioning your business for growth and success in this dynamic retail landscape.

Private Label Products

Private label products, often referred to as store brands or own brands, have become increasingly popular in the hardware industry. These products are created and sold exclusively by a particular retailer under their own brand name. Private label products offer a range of benefits for both retailers and consumers, and they play a significant role in the hardware store landscape.

One of the primary advantages of private label products is cost savings. Retailers can often produce private label goods at a lower cost compared to national or well-known brands. This cost efficiency allows retailers to offer these products to consumers at competitive prices, making them an attractive option for budget-conscious shoppers. Private label products also provide retailers with greater control over their product offerings. Retailers can tailor private label items to meet the specific preferences and demands of their target customer base. This customization allows for more flexibility in product development, ensuring that the products align with the store's brand image and customer needs.

Quality and value are key considerations for consumers when choosing private label products. Many retailers invest in stringent quality control and product testing to ensure that their private label items meet or exceed national brand standards. As a result, consumers often find private label products that offer a similar or even superior quality to their branded counterparts at a lower price point.

Private label products are not limited to any specific category; they can encompass a wide range of items, from food and beverages to household cleaning products and personal care items. This diversity allows retailers to create a comprehensive private label portfolio that covers various product categories, offering consumers an extensive selection of store brand choices.

In recent years, private label products have evolved beyond just budget-friendly options. Many retailers have introduced premium or gourmet private label lines that compete with higher-end national brands. This expansion allows retailers to cater to a broader spectrum of consumers and capture a larger share of the market.

Successful private label strategies require effective branding and marketing efforts. Retailers must create a strong brand identity for their private label products to build trust and loyalty among consumers. They often invest in packaging design, advertising, and promotional campaigns to showcase the value and quality of their store brand items.

Private label products have gained traction globally, and consumers are increasingly open to trying these offerings. The growth of e-commerce has also provided a platform for retailers to reach a wider audience with their private label products, making them even more accessible to consumers.

Private label products have become a significant and dynamic segment of the hardware industry. They offer cost savings, quality, and customization for retailers while providing consumers with value and choice. As retailers continue to innovate and invest in their private label portfolios, these products are likely to remain a prominent feature in the hardware store landscape.

Chapter 7:
Staffing and Management

Effective staffing and management are fundamental to the success of your hardware store. In this chapter, we will explore the key components of staffing and managing your hardware store, including the hiring and training of employees, the creation of employee policies, scheduling and shift management, and performance evaluation.

Hiring and Training Employees

When establishing a hardware store, having the right team of employees is crucial for providing excellent customer service, managing operations, and fostering a positive shopping experience. Consider the following roles and personnel needed:

Store Manager: An experienced store manager oversees daily operations, manages staff, handles inventory, ensures customer satisfaction, and implements business strategies. They play a pivotal role in maintaining the store's efficiency and profitability.

Sales Associates: Frontline sales associates assist customers, provide product information, process transactions, and maintain a neat and organized sales floor. They should possess excellent communication skills, product knowledge, and a customer-oriented approach.

Cashiers: Efficient cashiers handle transactions, process payments accurately, and provide customers with a positive checkout experience. They should be proficient in operating cash registers and handling various payment methods.

Inventory Manager: An inventory manager oversees stock levels, conducts inventory audits, manages orders, and ensures accurate tracking of merchandise. Their role is crucial in maintaining adequate inventory levels and preventing stock shortages.

Technical Experts: Employ individuals with specialized knowledge in hardware, tools, or specific trades. These experts can provide valuable advice to customers, offer guidance on product selection, and assist with technical queries.

Customer Service Representatives: Customer service representatives handle inquiries, resolve issues, and address customer concerns promptly and professionally. They serve as the liaison between customers and the store, ensuring a high level of satisfaction.

Maintenance Staff: Maintenance personnel ensure the store premises are clean, well-maintained, and adhere to safety standards. They handle repairs, upkeep of equipment, and manage facilities to create a safe and pleasant environment for customers and employees.

The process of hiring and training employees begins with a well-planned recruitment process aimed at attracting candidates who align with your store's values and customer service standards. Utilizing various channels such as online job boards, local newspapers, and social media, you can advertise job openings effectively. Additionally, consider hosting in-person or virtual job fairs to engage potential candidates.

Once you've identified suitable candidates, a rigorous selection process, including resume screening, interviews, reference checks, and skills assessments, ensures that you select employees who not only possess the necessary qualifications but also fit well within your store's culture. When recruiting, prioritize individuals with relevant industry experience, a customer-centric attitude, strong communication skills, and a willingness to learn and adapt. Following the hiring process, invest in comprehensive training programs that encompass on-the-job training and formal training sessions. These programs ensure that your staff members are well-versed in product offerings, customer service expectations, safety protocols, and store policies.

Creating Employee Policies

Establishing clear and comprehensive employee guidelines is key to a smooth and happy workplace. Start by crafting an employee handbook that serves as a go-to guide for your team. This handbook should cover everything from work schedules and dress code to attendance rules and performance expectations. Be sure to outline a code of conduct that lays out expected behavior and ethical standards for everyone, stressing the importance of respecting both customers and fellow colleagues.

It's crucial to implement policies against discrimination and harassment to foster a safe, inclusive environment. Make sure to clearly explain reporting procedures so that all employees know their rights and how they're protected.

Safety and health policies should be a top priority, making sure you're in line with local regulations and emphasizing the importance of a safe work environment. When it comes to compensation, lay out everything transparently—wage rates, overtime policies, benefits, and perks. And don't forget about attendance and punctuality guidelines, including how to request time off or report absences.

Additionally, it's essential to create policies for handling conflicts, providing a fair and confidential process for employees to address any issues with management or coworkers. Lastly, educate your team on respecting customer privacy and confidentiality, making sure they're clear on how to handle sensitive information appropriately.

Performance Evaluation

Performance evaluation is a pivotal aspect of managing your hardware store staff. Define key performance metrics for various roles within the store, including sales targets, customer service ratings, and productivity goals. Provide ongoing feedback to employees, helping them understand their strengths and areas for improvement. Encourage open dialogue and constructive feedback as part of your organizational culture.

Conduct regular performance reviews or evaluations to assess employee performance against established metrics and goals. Set aside dedicated time for these evaluations and involve employees in goal setting to align their individual objectives with the store's overall objectives. Recognize and reward outstanding performance through incentive programs, awards, or bonuses to motivate and retain high-performing employees.

Moreover, discuss career development opportunities with employees and provide guidance on how they can advance within the organization. Offer training and support for career growth, demonstrating your commitment to their professional development. In cases where employees are not meeting performance expectations, develop performance improvement plans that outline specific steps for improvement. Offer support and resources to help employees succeed while also being prepared to take appropriate action, including termination, if performance issues persist despite efforts to address them.

Managing staffing and employee performance is an ongoing process that demands attention to detail, effective communication, and a commitment to fostering a positive work environment. By hiring and training employees effectively, creating clear policies, managing schedules efficiently, and conducting performance evaluations, you can build a motivated and capable team that contributes significantly to the success of your hardware store.

Chapter 8:
Marketing and Promotion

In the hardware industry, a well-crafted marketing and promotion strategy is essential to attract and retain customers, create a strong brand presence, and drive sales. In this chapter, we will explore the key components of effective marketing and promotion for your hardware store, including developing a marketing plan, establishing your store's branding and image, implementing advertising and promotion strategies, and utilizing loyalty programs to foster customer loyalty and engagement.

Developing a Marketing Plan

A marketing plan serves as the guiding blueprint for a hardware store's promotional activities, providing a structured approach to achieving desired outcomes. To develop a comprehensive marketing plan, several key steps should be followed.

Conducting Market Research

Market research forms the cornerstone of an effective marketing strategy for your hardware store. It's the vital process of gathering information that unveils the thoughts, purchasing behaviors, and geographical presence of your customers.

This research isn't just about understanding your customers; it's also a tool to craft an initial sales forecast, track market shifts, and keenly observe your competitors' actions.

By delving into market research, you'll gain valuable insights into what drives your customers' decisions, where they are located, and how they engage with hardware products. This knowledge becomes the bedrock upon which you can build a robust marketing strategy that resonates with your target audience, identifies growth opportunities, and sets your store apart from the competition.

Whether it's analyzing buying patterns, gauging customer preferences, or staying updated on industry trends, market research empowers your hardware store to make informed decisions and stay ahead in a dynamic market landscape.

Profiling Your Target Markets

Attempting to reach everyone with your hardware products can drain resources and yield minimal impact. Instead, focusing your marketing efforts through segmentation can be a game-changer. By grouping potential customers based on specific characteristics, you can refine and tailor your marketing strategies for maximum effectiveness.

Here are key segmentation factors to consider:

Geography: Understand where your customers live and work. This insight helps tailor your marketing approach to specific regions or areas.

Demographics: Consider gender, age, education level, occupation, and income. These details paint a clearer picture of your customer base and aid in crafting targeted messages.

Behavior: Why would they use your products? What draws them to your brand? Understanding usage rates and their preferred information sources guides how you communicate and engage with them.

Lifestyle and Values: Delve into their family situation, values, hobbies, and interests. Knowing these aspects helps align your marketing messages with what matters most to them.

Your ideal target market should not only require your hardware offerings but also be willing to invest in them. Understanding their needs, preferences, and behaviors empowers you to tailor your marketing efforts effectively. By honing in on specific customer segments, your hardware store can deliver tailored solutions that resonate deeply with these diverse groups, fostering stronger connections and driving more impactful results.

Crafting Your Unique Selling Proposition (USP)

Your hardware store's USP is the distinctive factor that sets you apart from competitors and entices customers to choose you over others. It's the essence of what makes your business shine in a crowded market. Defining and effectively communicating your USP is key to captivating potential customers.

To develop your USP, consider the following:

Passion for Products and Services: What excites you the most about your offerings? Your genuine enthusiasm often translates into a unique selling point. Whether it's the quality, variety, or innovation, conveying your passion can be magnetic.

Specialized Skills and Knowledge: Identify the unique expertise or knowledge your team possesses. This could be technical know-how, expert guidance, or a deep understanding of specific products—factors that differentiate you from the competition.

Customer Draw: Why do customers choose you over others? Understanding this helps define your USP. Whether it's exceptional service, a loyalty program, or a personalized approach, pinpoint what consistently attracts customers to your store.

Customer Benefits: Highlight the tangible advantages your customers gain by choosing your products or services. Whether it's convenience, reliability, cost-effectiveness, or solving specific problems, emphasize how customers benefit from their association with your store.

Key Messaging: When describing your business to strangers, what aspects do you emphasize? These points often align with your USP. Whether it's outstanding customer support, exclusive product lines, or a commitment to quality, these aspects become pivotal in shaping your USP's narrative.

By analyzing these aspects, you can distill your hardware store's unique strengths into a compelling USP. This proposition becomes the backbone of your marketing efforts, guiding your messaging, and resonating strongly with potential customers, ultimately setting you apart and driving customer loyalty and engagement.

Developing Your Business Brand
Creating a brand for your hardware store is a comprehensive endeavor that involves more than just the visual elements like logos and colors. It's about establishing a meaningful connection with your target audience. A well-crafted brand goes beyond surface-level aesthetics; it's a means to communicate your core values, your identity, and what customers can expect from your store.

Choose Your Marketing Media
When it comes to marketing your hardware store, the array of avenues available can be overwhelming. However, it's crucial to align your choices with your target audience to maximize their effectiveness.

Consider these options:

Business Website: Establishing an online presence through a website allows potential customers to explore your offerings, services, and values. It's a digital storefront that can attract and engage customers.

Social Media: Platforms like Facebook, Instagram, or LinkedIn offer opportunities to connect with your audience on a more personal level. Engaging content and interaction can build a community around your brand.

Blogging: Creating informative and valuable content through a blog can position your store as an authority in the hardware industry. It's a way to share expertise and attract customers seeking guidance.

Brochures and Flyers: Tangible marketing materials can be effective in local promotions or events. They provide a physical reminder of your store and offerings.

Networking Events: Engaging in industry-related events or local gatherings can help forge connections and establish your store within the community.

Print Advertising: Traditional print media, like newspapers or magazines, can still reach a specific demographic effectively, especially in localized markets.

Word of Mouth: Encourage satisfied customers to spread the word about your store. Positive recommendations can be a powerful driver for new customers.

Cold Calling: Direct outreach can be effective in B2B sales or when targeting specific customer segments. It's a proactive way to introduce your store and offerings.

Email Marketing: Sending targeted and personalized emails can nurture customer relationships, share promotions, and keep your store top-of-mind.

By understanding your target audience's preferences and behaviors, you can select the most fitting marketing avenues for your hardware store. Each avenue offers distinct opportunities to engage with customers, amplify your brand, and drive sales, so tailoring your approach to match your audience's preferences is key to maximizing your marketing efforts.

Establishing Goals and Allocating Budget for Your Marketing
Defining clear and concise marketing goals is pivotal for guiding your hardware store's growth. These goals should adhere to the SMART criteria—specific, measurable, attainable, relevant, and time-based.

Consider setting goals such as increasing website traffic by a certain percentage, boosting social media engagement, or enhancing sales of specific product categories within a defined timeframe. These objectives provide direction and allow for effective evaluation of your marketing efforts.

For a hardware store, these SMART objectives could encompass various goals:

- Increasing Sales: Define a specific percentage increase in sales within a set timeframe.
- Expanding Market Share: Set a goal to capture a certain percentage of the local hardware market within a year.

- Launching a New Store Location: Outline specific steps and targets to successfully launch a new store, including a timeline for pre-launch marketing, opening day sales, and post-launch growth.

Allocating a budget is equally crucial. Your marketing budget needs to encompass various elements essential for promoting your hardware store effectively. It should cover:

Website Development and Maintenance: Investing in a professional and user-friendly website is fundamental. Regular maintenance ensures it remains up-to-date and functional.

Search Engine Optimization (SEO) Strategy: Optimizing your online presence to rank higher in search engine results is vital for visibility. Allocate resources for SEO tools and strategies to enhance your store's online discoverability.

Branding Design: Designing a compelling brand identity, including logos, color schemes, and visual elements that resonate with your target audience.

Printing of Promotional Material: Costs related to producing business cards, brochures, signage, and other promotional materials that represent your store's image.

Advertising Costs: Funding for advertising campaigns across various platforms, whether digital, print, or local media.

Donations and Sponsorships: Consider community involvement through donations or sponsorships that align with your brand values and foster positive relationships.

Staff for Marketing Activities: Allocating resources for employing or training staff dedicated to marketing activities, ensuring a focused approach towards achieving marketing goals.

By establishing SMART goals and earmarking a comprehensive budget covering these critical marketing elements, your hardware store can strategically channel resources towards initiatives that align with your business objectives. This disciplined approach enhances the effectiveness of your marketing endeavors, leading to tangible results and the sustained growth of your store.

Nurturing Your Valued Customers

Your customers are the backbone of your hardware store's success, making it imperative to prioritize their care and loyalty. Exceptional customer service isn't just a bonus—it's a crucial factor that retains customers and sets you apart from competitors.

Here are strategies to cultivate customer loyalty:

Regular Communication: Engage customers consistently through social media, blogs, or e-newsletters. Providing valuable content and updates keeps your store top-of-mind.

After-Sale Follow-Up: Show your commitment by following up after a sale. Checking in on their satisfaction and offering support builds a lasting impression.

Delivering on Promises: Consistently meeting or exceeding promises made to customers establishes trust and reliability.

Going the Extra Mile: Surprise and delight your customers by providing benefits that surpass their initial expectations. It could be personalized recommendations, exclusive discounts, or exceptional service that leaves a lasting positive impression.

Utilizing Feedback: Embrace feedback and complaints as opportunities to enhance your services. Actively listening and implementing necessary improvements demonstrate your dedication to customer satisfaction.

Listening Intently: Take the time to genuinely listen to your customers. Understanding their needs and concerns helps tailor your services to meet their expectations effectively.

Staff Training: Invest in training your staff in customer service and sales processes. Equipping them with the skills to engage customers positively enhances the overall experience.

By implementing these strategies, your hardware store can foster a loyal customer base. Consistently providing exceptional service, actively listening to feedback, and going beyond expectations help create a strong bond with customers. This dedication not only encourages repeat business but also turns satisfied customers into enthusiastic advocates, driving positive word-of-mouth and contributing significantly to your store's long-term success.

Monitoring and Reviewing Marketing Effort

Regularly monitoring and assessing your marketing initiatives is crucial to ensure they align with your goals and deliver the desired outcomes, such as increased sales or heightened brand visibility. Initially, it's recommended to review your marketing plan every three months to ensure your activities are in sync with your overall strategy. As your business matures, consider reviewing the plan when introducing new products/services, encountering new competitors, or facing industry-related challenges.

Monitoring activities involves various assessments, such as regularly analyzing sales figures (monthly) or tracking customer engagement during advertising campaigns. Leveraging free analytic tools enables you to evaluate the effectiveness of your social media or website campaigns.

By routinely evaluating the performance of your marketing efforts, you can gain valuable insights into what strategies are yielding positive results and which ones may need adjustments. This process helps in optimizing your marketing activities, reallocating resources to high-performing channels, and refining strategies to better resonate with your target audience.

Additionally, staying vigilant regarding shifts in the market, new industry trends, or changes in customer behavior enables you to adapt swiftly. By continuously monitoring and reviewing your marketing plan, your hardware store remains agile and responsive to evolving market conditions, ensuring sustained growth and success in the competitive landscape.

Branding and Store Image

Branding encompasses more than just a logo and a catchy slogan; it represents the essence of your hardware store's identity. Building a strong brand image is not only essential for setting your store apart from competitors but also for fostering customer trust and leaving a lasting impression. To create a compelling brand identity, follow these essential steps:

Define Your Brand: The process begins by clearly defining your store's values, mission, and vision. What is it that you want your hardware store to stand for, and what unique qualities will distinguish it from others in the market?

Logo and Visual Identity: Craft a memorable logo and visual identity that align with your brand's personality and values. It's crucial to ensure consistency in these branding elements across all marketing materials and in-store signage.

Store Layout and Design: The interior design and layout of your store should seamlessly align with your brand image. The atmosphere, color schemes, and decor should vividly convey your brand's values and resonate with your target audience.

Customer Experience: Delivering a consistent and exceptional customer experience is pivotal to upholding your brand promise. Train your staff to embody your brand values in their interactions with customers, creating a lasting impression.

Brand Messaging: Develop compelling brand messaging that effectively communicates your store's unique selling points and resonates with your intended audience. Maintain the consistency of this messaging across all communication channels.

Brand Voice: Cultivate a consistent brand voice that reflects your brand's personality. Whether it's a friendly, informative, or humorous tone, ensure that it remains aligned with your brand image.

Community Engagement: Actively engage with the local community and support causes that align with your brand values. Sponsoring local events, participating in charity initiatives, or contributing to environmental efforts can enhance your brand's reputation and foster a sense of community.

Feedback and Adaptation: Continuously seek feedback from your customers to gain insights into their perceptions of your brand. Be willing to adapt and evolve your brand identity in response to changing customer preferences and market trends.

In essence, branding and store image creation involve a holistic approach that encompasses visual identity, messaging, atmosphere, and customer experience. By meticulously crafting and nurturing your brand, you can establish a distinct and memorable identity in the hardware market, leading to increased customer loyalty and trust.

Promoting Your Store

Getting the word out about your hardware store is essential, and fortunately, today's landscape offers a myriad of promotional avenues. Traditional business promotion methods remain effective, but the surge of social media has opened up a wealth of new marketing opportunities. Embracing digital marketing and social media can present affordable and accessible advertising options for your store. Here's how to leverage these tools to promote your business effectively:

Maximize Local Exposure

Harness the power of local listings by ensuring your hardware store is listed on Google—a modern-day equivalent to the classic yellow pages. Registering your business with Google offers numerous advantages, allowing potential customers to effortlessly locate your store's address and operating hours.

Here's why setting up a Google My Business account is pivotal:

Enhanced Visibility: A Google My Business account significantly boosts your store's online visibility. When users search for hardware stores in your area, your business will appear prominently in search results, increasing your chances of attracting local customers.

Ease of Access: Providing essential information such as your store's location, hours of operation, contact details, and even directions on Google Maps simplifies the process for customers to find and reach your store easily.

Customer Engagement: Google My Business facilitates customer engagement by enabling customers to post reviews and ratings of your hardware store. Positive reviews can enhance your store's reputation and influence potential customers' decisions.

Free Advertising: Utilizing Google My Business is essentially a form of free advertising. It extends your store's reach without incurring additional costs, making it a cost-effective way to increase your store's visibility online.

By setting up a Google My Business account, your hardware store can leverage the vast reach of Google's search engine to connect with local customers actively seeking hardware solutions. This simple yet powerful tool not only enhances your store's visibility but also facilitates customer engagement and trust, ultimately driving foot traffic and boosting your store's success in the local market.

Create a Truthworthy Website
Establishing a reliable online presence is vital for your hardware store. Your website should serve as a comprehensive hub showcasing your services, products, and the essence of your hardware ethos. It's not just about listing services; it's about conveying your hardware philosophy. Offer a seamless booking platform and foster communication with customers. Remember, your website often forms the initial impression of your store, so ensure it mirrors your brand values. Explore top hardware store websites for inspiration on how to best represent your business online.

Enhance Your Website with SEO Optimization

Boosting your hardware store's online visibility begins with optimizing your website's search engine optimization (SEO). SEO is the key to securing higher rankings in Google searches, making it easier for potential customers to discover your business online. While integrating relevant keywords across your web pages and blog posts is vital, effective SEO involves more than just keyword usage.

To optimize your website's performance on search engines, consider these steps:

Keyword Integration: Strategically incorporate relevant keywords throughout your website's content, ensuring they align with the products, services, and solutions your hardware store offers. Use tools or online resources to identify high-impact keywords for your industry.

Content Quality: Focus on creating high-quality, informative content that addresses common queries or issues within the hardware and home improvement sphere. Well-crafted content not only engages visitors but also attracts search engine attention.

Technical Optimization: Ensure your website is technically sound by optimizing loading speeds, mobile responsiveness, and user experience. A seamless browsing experience enhances your site's ranking potential.

Research and Learning: Expand your knowledge by exploring online resources or educational materials dedicated to mastering SEO techniques. Understanding the nuances of effective SEO practices can significantly impact your website's performance.

Professional Assistance: Consider hiring an SEO agency or consultant specialized in optimizing websites. Their expertise can offer tailored strategies to enhance your site's SEO, saving time and ensuring effective results.

By embracing SEO best practices, your hardware store's website can rise through search engine rankings, attracting more organic traffic and potential customers. A well-optimized website not only improves visibility but also establishes credibility and trust among online users, ultimately contributing to the success and growth of your hardware store in the competitive digital landscape.

Leveraging Social Media

Social media has evolved from a mere option to a crucial necessity for businesses. These platforms offer a dynamic space to inform, attract, and actively engage with your audience. Setting up a business account on most social media sites is entirely free, making it an incredibly cost-effective means of advertising for your hardware store. While creating paid posts and other forms of social media ads require an investment, the initial setup remains accessible to all.

By establishing a presence on platforms like Facebook, Instagram, Twitter, or LinkedIn, your hardware store gains direct access to a vast audience. Through regular posts, stories, and interactions, you can showcase your products, share valuable insights, and build a community around your brand. These platforms also facilitate two-way communication, allowing you to respond promptly to inquiries, address concerns, and foster meaningful connections with your followers.

Paid social media posts and advertisements offer additional advantages by targeting specific demographics, boosting visibility, and driving traffic to your store or website. Though these strategies involve a financial investment, they often yield measurable returns by reaching a tailored audience likely to engage with your hardware offerings.

Social media's versatility, accessibility, and potential to reach a wide audience make it an indispensable tool for your hardware store's advertising efforts. From establishing brand presence to engaging with customers and running targeted ad campaigns, leveraging social media enables your store to stay competitive, relevant, and connected in today's digital landscape.

Craft Compelling Content

Content stands as the linchpin for amplifying brand awareness and forging connections with your desired audience. Creating compelling and informative content—be it through blogs, video tutorials, or engaging infographics—serves as a powerful tool to showcase your hardware store's industry expertise and foster trust among your audience.

Blogs: Share valuable insights, tips, and trends related to hardware, home improvement, or DIY projects. Informative blog posts not only exhibit your knowledge but also provide practical guidance that resonates with your audience's interests and needs.

Video Tutorials: Capitalize on the visual medium by producing step-by-step video tutorials showcasing product demonstrations, repair techniques, or innovative uses of hardware items. These tutorials not only exhibit your expertise but also serve as valuable resources for your customers.

Infographics: Condense complex information into visually appealing and easily digestible infographics. Highlight product comparisons, maintenance tips, or creative project ideas.

Infographics serve as shareable content that can attract and engage your audience effectively.

By consistently crafting engaging and informative content, your hardware store can position itself as a trusted authority within the industry. This approach not only cultivates a deeper connection with your audience but also encourages them to view your store as a go-to resource for their hardware needs. As you offer valuable insights and guidance, you simultaneously bolster brand recognition and loyalty, fostering lasting relationships with your customers.

Use High-Quality Visuals
Visual content is the cornerstone of a compelling online presence. For your hardware store, investing in high-quality visual content for your website and social media platforms is paramount. In today's digital landscape, users often make decisions based on visuals, making it imperative to showcase your store in its best light.

Consider incorporating photos or videos that spotlight your products, services, facilities, and even your staff. High-resolution images showcasing the details and features of your hardware products can captivate potential customers, influencing their buying decisions. Additionally, videos demonstrating the usage or benefits of specific tools or equipment can be incredibly engaging and informative.

On social media, where attention spans are shorter, visually appealing content stands out. Striking images or eye-catching videos are more likely to capture users' attention and encourage engagement. Visuals have the power to convey your store's personality, professionalism, and the value you offer to customers.

Moreover, high-quality visuals not only attract attention but also contribute to establishing credibility and trust. They showcase your dedication to quality and attention to detail, which can resonate positively with your audience.

By prioritizing high-quality visual content across your online platforms, you're not just showcasing your hardware store; you're creating an immersive and compelling experience that entices potential customers to explore your offerings further. Visuals serve as a powerful tool to communicate the uniqueness and value of your store, setting you apart and fostering a strong connection with your audience.

Participate in Local and Community Events
For a hardware store deeply rooted in the local community, participating in both virtual and in-person events holds immense value. These gatherings offer prime opportunities to connect with your target audience, network with fellow business owners, and engage directly with potential customers, creating meaningful interactions that go beyond traditional advertising.

By actively participating in local events, you position your hardware store in the heart of the community, fostering relationships and strengthening your brand presence. Here's how these events can benefit your business:

Networking Opportunities: Events provide a platform to meet and collaborate with other local business owners, fostering partnerships that can mutually benefit each other's endeavors.

Direct Customer Interaction: Engaging with prospective customers face-to-face allows for personal connections. It's an ideal setting to showcase your products, share expertise, and address inquiries, thereby building trust and credibility.

Promotional Platform: Use these events as a promotional avenue to highlight special offers, exclusive deals, or upcoming products. Create a booth or display that captivates attendees and showcases the uniqueness of your hardware store.

Community Integration: Participation in local events signifies your store's commitment to the community. It's an opportunity to support community initiatives, establish goodwill, and solidify your store's position as a valued local establishment.

Whether it's setting up a booth at a local fair, sponsoring a community event, or engaging in online forums, actively participating in local and community events aligns your hardware store with the community's pulse. It's a chance to connect personally, forge meaningful relationships, and imprint your brand in the minds of local residents, ultimately contributing to long-term loyalty and success within your community.

Paid Advertising Strategies

If you're aiming to expand your hardware store's reach rapidly, investing in paid advertising can be a game-changer. Here are some popular paid advertising methods to consider:

Television and Radio Ads: While a traditional approach, TV and radio ads offer extensive reach. They cover a broader audience but typically involve higher costs compared to other methods.

Promoted Social Media Posts: Transforming one of your store's social media posts into an ad allows for targeted promotion. You have the flexibility to select a specific audience, geographic region, and duration for running the ad. This method ensures your content reaches those most likely to engage with it.

Pay-Per-Click (PPC) Ads: This model charges you each time a user clicks on your ad. Platforms like Google offer PPC advertising, displaying your ad prominently at the top of search engine results for specific keywords you've chosen. It's a cost-effective way to target users actively searching for hardware-related products or services.

Each of these paid advertising methods offers distinct advantages. Television and radio ads provide broad exposure, while promoted social media posts and PPC ads enable precise targeting, ensuring your message reaches the most relevant audience.

By strategically investing in paid advertising that aligns with your hardware store's goals and target demographic, you can amplify visibility, drive traffic to your store, and generate valuable leads, ultimately contributing to the growth and success of your business.

Engage Your Audience with Workshops and Offers

As a hardware store looking to make a mark, consider hosting workshops or webinars to share your expertise and solidify your position as a knowledgeable authority in your field. These sessions, whether online or in person, serve as invaluable platforms to impart specialized skills or technical know-how. By sharing valuable insights, you not only educate prospective customers but also establish meaningful connections within your industry. Additionally, these workshops present an opportunity to collect contact information from attendees, nurturing relationships for potential future business.

Another effective strategy is offering discounted or free products/services. Introductory discounts and complimentary trials act as enticing incentives for new customers, sparking their interest in your offerings. Encouraging referrals through customer-exclusive deals can amplify your customer base while fostering a sense of loyalty. Moreover, providing free samples or trials allows prospective customers to experience the quality of your products or services without a financial commitment. This approach builds trust and allows your offerings to speak for themselves, creating a strong foundation for future business relationships.

Remember, combining these strategies can amplify their impact. Investing in your business dreams is crucial, and a business banking expert can guide you on leveraging a business banking account to maximize your business's potential. By integrating these tactics, your hardware store can elevate its visibility, foster trust with customers, and establish a solid foothold in the market, paving the way for sustained growth and success.

Chapter 9:
Operations and Logistics

Efficient operations and logistics are the backbone of a successful hardware store. In this chapter, we will explore the intricacies of managing daily store operations, optimizing supply chain management, controlling inventory, and ensuring quality assurance to deliver a seamless shopping experience to your customers.

Daily Store Operations

Running a successful hardware store involves a multitude of daily tasks and responsibilities that demand meticulous planning and execution. These operational processes are the backbone of the store's efficiency and customer satisfaction. Here's an overview of essential daily store operations:

Store Opening and Closing: Establishing clear opening and closing procedures is paramount to ensuring the seamless commencement and conclusion of each business day. These procedures encompass tasks such as securely unlocking and locking the premises, setting up enticing displays, and conducting closing inventory counts to maintain inventory accuracy.

Staff Scheduling: Crafting a well-structured daily staff schedule is critical for maintaining optimal staffing levels, especially during peak business hours. Efficient allocation of staff resources not only guarantees excellent customer service but also minimizes labor costs, contributing to overall operational effectiveness.

Customer Service: Prioritize customer service excellence by providing extensive training to your staff. This training should encompass welcoming and assisting customers, addressing their inquiries promptly, and ensuring a consistently pleasant shopping experience that fosters customer loyalty.

Checkout Process: Streamlining the checkout process is essential to minimize waiting times for customers. Implement efficient point-of-sale (POS) systems and provide comprehensive training to cashiers to facilitate swift and accurate transaction processing, enhancing customer satisfaction.

Store Maintenance: Regularly inspecting and maintaining the store's physical premises is crucial. This entails tasks such as routine cleaning, equipment maintenance, and promptly addressing any safety hazards to create a safe and pleasant shopping environment.

Merchandising: Ensuring that products are displayed attractively and that shelves remain well-stocked is pivotal in maximizing sales and customer engagement. Frequent restocking and strategic visual merchandising contribute to a dynamic and enticing shopping experience.

Order Fulfillment: If your store offers online and phone orders, it's imperative to efficiently manage order fulfillment. Timely processing and delivery or pickup of customer orders are essential for ensuring high levels of customer satisfaction and repeat business.

Security: Implementing comprehensive security measures, including surveillance cameras, alarms, and loss prevention strategies, is vital to protect against theft and to ensure the safety of both customers and employees. A secure shopping environment enhances customer trust.

Waste Management: Develop a robust waste management plan to effectively handle and dispose of both perishable and nonperishable items. This includes implementing recycling practices and adhering to environmental regulations, aligning your store with sustainable practices and responsible waste disposal.

The daily operations of a hardware store are multifaceted and intricately interconnected. Effective management of these operations is pivotal in providing outstanding customer experiences, maintaining store efficiency, and ensuring the overall success of the business.

Supply Chain Management

Supply chain management plays a crucial role in the efficient and effective operation of a hardware store. It involves the planning, coordination, and control of the flow of goods and information from suppliers to the store's shelves, with the ultimate goal of meeting customer demand while minimizing costs and maximizing profitability.

One of the key aspects of supply chain management for a hardware store is vendor selection and management. Choosing reliable and cost-effective suppliers is essential to ensure a steady and high-quality supply of products. Hardware stores often work with a variety of suppliers, including wholesalers, and distributors, to source products, packaged goods, and other items. Establishing strong relationships with these suppliers can lead to better pricing, timely deliveries, and access to unique products that can give the store a competitive edge.

Inventory management is another critical component of supply chain management for a hardware store. Balancing inventory levels to meet customer demand while avoiding overstocking or understocking is a delicate task. Advanced inventory management systems and technologies can help store managers track product levels in real-time, forecast demand, and automatically reorder products when necessary. This reduces the risk of product spoilage, stockouts, and excess inventory, which can eat into profits.

Efficient transportation and logistics are vital for ensuring that products move smoothly from suppliers to the hardware store's shelves. Hardware stores often have multiple distribution centers to receive and distribute products to individual store locations. Optimizing routes, scheduling deliveries, and using technology like GPS tracking can help reduce transportation costs and ensure on-time deliveries. Moreover, eco-friendly transportation practices can align with sustainability goals and reduce the store's carbon footprint.

In today's highly competitive retail landscape, data analytics and technology play an increasingly significant role in supply chain management for hardware stores. Collecting and analyzing data on customer preferences, sales trends, and inventory turnover can help stores make informed decisions about product assortment, pricing, and promotions. The use of RFID tags, barcodes, and advanced software systems can enhance inventory visibility, reduce errors, and streamline the replenishment process.

Effective supply chain management is essential for the success of a hardware store. It involves vendor selection, inventory management, transportation, technology, data analytics, and compliance with safety regulations. By optimizing these aspects of the supply chain, hardware stores can enhance customer satisfaction, reduce costs, and remain competitive in a dynamic and evolving retail industry.

Inventory Control

Inventory control is a crucial element of supply chain management that plays a pivotal role in various industries. It refers to the processes and strategies utilized by organizations to efficiently manage their stock of goods. Effective inventory control is essential for ensuring product availability, reducing carrying costs, avoiding stockouts, and optimizing overall business operations.

One of the primary objectives of inventory control is to find the right equilibrium between maintaining sufficient stock levels to meet customer demand and minimizing excess inventory. Excessive inventory can tie up valuable capital and storage space, increasing the risks of obsolescence and spoilage. Conversely, insufficient inventory can lead to stockouts, resulting in lost sales and customer dissatisfaction. Businesses employ inventory control methods to determine optimal stock levels for each product, relying on historical sales data, demand forecasts, and lead times.

Accurate and up-to-date record-keeping is fundamental to effective inventory control. This entails tracking the quantity, value, location, and movements of every item in the inventory. Modern businesses often utilize computerized inventory management systems that automate these tasks, offering real-time visibility into stock levels and facilitating rapid decision-making. These systems can generate reports on stock turnover rates, reorder points, and supplier performance, facilitating inventory control efforts.

The ABC analysis is a fundamental concept in inventory control, classifying products into categories based on their significance and value. "A" items represent high-value, high-priority products requiring meticulous monitoring and tighter control. "B" items hold moderate importance, while "C" items are low-value, low-priority products. This categorization enables businesses to allocate resources effectively, focusing efforts on managing the most critical items.

Inventory control strategies encompass various techniques for managing demand fluctuations and uncertainties. Safety stock, for instance, involves maintaining a buffer of extra inventory to account for unexpected demand surges or supply delays. Reorder points and economic order quantity (EOQ) calculations help determine when to reorder products to maintain desired stock levels while minimizing carrying costs. Just-in-time (JIT) inventory systems take an alternative approach, aiming to minimize inventory holding costs by receiving goods from suppliers precisely when needed.

Effective inventory control yields numerous benefits for businesses. It can reduce carrying costs associated with storage, insurance, and handling. It helps prevent overstocking, which ties up capital, and understocking, which results in missed sales opportunities. Furthermore, it contributes to stronger supplier relationships by providing accurate demand forecasts and ensuring timely replenishment orders.

Inventory control is an indispensable practice within supply chain management, aimed at striking a balance between optimal stock levels and minimal carrying costs. It involves the application of techniques such as ABC analysis, safety stock, EOQ, and JIT to streamline inventory management. By implementing effective inventory control strategies, businesses can enhance their overall efficiency, customer satisfaction, and financial performance.

Quality Assurance

Maintaining product quality is paramount in the hardware business. Quality assurance measures help ensure that customers receive safe and fresh products:

Quality Standards: Establish and communicate clear quality standards for all products, including freshness, appearance, and packaging.

Vendor Compliance: Work closely with suppliers to ensure they adhere to quality and safety standards. Regularly audit and assess supplier practices.

Regular Inspections: Conduct routine inspections of products, checking for any signs of spoilage, damage, or expiration.

Employee Training: Train employees on proper handling and storage of products to maintain quality throughout the supply chain.

Recall Procedures: Develop clear procedures for handling product recalls. Communicate recalls to customers promptly and efficiently.

Efficient operations and logistics, coupled with a strong focus on quality assurance, are essential for the success and sustainability of your hardware store. By carefully managing daily operations, optimizing your supply chain, controlling inventory, and ensuring product quality, you can provide a seamless shopping experience that keeps customers coming back.

Chapter 10:
Growth and Expansion

Expanding your hardware store business is a significant step toward increasing profitability and market presence. In this chapter, we'll explore various strategies for growth and expansion, including broadening your product line, opening additional locations, considering franchising opportunities, and exploring international expansion.

Expanding Your Product Line

Diversifying your product offerings can breathe new life into your hardware store and attract a broader customer base. Here's how to approach expanding your product line. begin with thorough market research to identify products in demand within your community. This step involves considering customer surveys, analyzing market trends, and assessing competitor offerings. By understanding what your customers want and what's currently popular, you can make informed decisions about which products to add to your inventory.

Strengthening your relationships with existing suppliers is crucial, and also seek out new ones to source the additional products you plan to offer. Building strong supplier partnerships ensures a consistent and reliable supply of new items, helping you maintain the quality and availability of your expanded product line.

As you expand your product line, it's essential to revise your inventory management strategies. This includes reevaluating your storage capacity, shelving layouts, and tracking systems. Adequate storage and efficient organization are key to managing a more diverse inventory effectively.

Your employees play a vital role in the success of your expanded product line. Ensure your staff is knowledgeable about the new products and can assist customers with inquiries. Consider providing specialized training where necessary to enhance their expertise and confidence when dealing with the new offerings.

Creating effective marketing campaigns is crucial to introducing the new products to your customer base. Utilize a mix of strategies, including in-store displays, digital advertising, and promotional events, to generate interest and inform your customers about the exciting additions to your inventory.

Once the new products are on the shelves, continuously gather customer feedback. This valuable input allows you to fine-tune your offerings and make adjustments based on customer preferences. Listening to your customers and responding to their needs helps ensure the long-term success of your expanded product line.

Expanding your product line can be a strategic move to grow your hardware store business. However, it should be approached systematically, with careful consideration of market research, supplier relationships, inventory management, employee training, marketing efforts, and ongoing customer feedback. By following these steps, you can effectively diversify your product offerings and attract a wider customer base while maintaining customer satisfaction and profitability.

Opening Additional Locations

Expanding your hardware store by opening additional locations can significantly increase your reach and market share. However, this endeavor involves a series of crucial considerations to ensure a successful expansion.

Location Selection: One of the most critical factors in opening new hardware store locations is selecting the right spot. Conduct thorough location analysis to identify areas with high foot traffic, underserved markets, or demographics that align with your target customer base. Understanding the local market dynamics and competition is essential in making an informed decision.

Legal and Regulatory Requirements: Before proceeding with a new location, it's vital to navigate the legal and regulatory landscape. Ensure you understand and comply with local zoning laws, permits, and regulations specific to the hardware retail industry. Failing to do so can lead to costly delays and complications.

Financial Planning: Create a comprehensive financial plan for the new location. This plan should include detailed projections of startup costs, operating expenses, and revenue expectations. Securing the necessary financing or capital to fund the expansion is essential to ensure a smooth launch and sustained growth.

Staffing: The success of a new store often hinges on the quality and readiness of your staff. Begin the hiring and training process well in advance of the opening to ensure that the team is adequately prepared to serve customers and manage operations. Consistency in service quality across all locations is key to maintaining your brand's reputation.

Supply Chain Management: Expanding to additional locations requires a reevaluation of your supply chain and logistics operations. Consider centralizing warehousing and distribution to ensure consistent product availability across all stores. Efficient supply chain management is crucial for minimizing costs and ensuring product freshness.

Marketing and Branding: Developing a solid marketing strategy is essential to introduce the new location to the community. Leverage your existing brand identity, but be prepared to customize it to the local market. Tailoring your marketing efforts to reflect the unique characteristics and preferences of the new location can help build a loyal customer base.

Monitoring and Evaluation: After opening, continuously monitor the performance of the new location. Establish key performance indicators (KPIs) to assess its success and compare it to your initial projections. Be prepared to make adjustments to operations, marketing, and staffing based on the data and feedback received to ensure the ongoing success of the new store.

In conclusion, opening additional locations for your hardware store can be a rewarding strategy for growth, but it requires careful planning and execution. By addressing location selection, legal requirements, financial planning, staffing, supply chain management, marketing, and ongoing evaluation, you can increase your chances of a successful expansion and enhance your market presence.

Franchising Opportunities

Franchising opportunities offer a unique avenue for business expansion and growth. This business model allows entrepreneurs to replicate a successful and established brand, concept, or product by licensing the rights to operate under the parent company's name and guidance. Here, we delve into the key aspects of franchising opportunities.

One of the primary advantages of franchising is the ability to tap into a proven business model. Franchisors typically have a track record of success, a well-developed business plan, and a strong brand identity. This can reduce the risks associated with starting a new business from scratch and increase the likelihood of profitability.

For entrepreneurs, franchising offers a level of independence while still benefiting from the support and resources of an established brand. Franchisees can leverage the franchisor's expertise in areas such as marketing, operations, and supply chain management. This support can be especially beneficial for individuals who may have limited experience in running a business.

Franchising opportunities also come with a ready-made customer base. Established brands often have a loyal following, which can translate into a steady stream of customers from day one. This can significantly reduce the time and effort required to build brand recognition and attract customers.

However, it's crucial for potential franchisees to carefully evaluate the terms and conditions of the franchise agreement. Franchise agreements outline the responsibilities and obligations of both the franchisor and the franchisee. These agreements often include details about fees, royalties, territorial restrictions, and operational standards. Prospective franchisees should seek legal and financial advice to ensure they fully understand the terms before committing.

Franchising opportunities extend to various industries, from fast food and retail to fitness centers and service businesses. The choice of franchise should align with the interests, skills, and financial capacity of the potential franchisee. Conducting thorough market research and due diligence is essential to select the right franchise that matches one's goals and resources.

Once a franchise is established, ongoing communication and collaboration between the franchisor and franchisee are critical.

Franchisees benefit from regular training, updates on best practices, and support in addressing operational challenges. Franchisors, in turn, rely on franchisees to maintain the brand's reputation and uphold quality standards.

In conclusion, franchising opportunities provide a pathway for entrepreneurs to enter the business world with the backing of an established brand and support structure. It offers a balance between independence and guidance, making it an appealing option for those looking to start their own businesses. However, due diligence and a clear understanding of the franchise agreement are essential to ensure a successful and mutually beneficial partnership between franchisor and franchisee.

Each of these growth and expansion strategies comes with its own set of opportunities and challenges. The choice of which path to pursue should align with your business goals, resources, and risk tolerance. Careful planning, market research, and a commitment to maintaining the quality and values of your hardware store are essential elements of successful growth and expansion in the highly competitive hardware industry.

Conclusion

Starting and running a successful hardware store is a challenging but rewarding endeavor. In this comprehensive guide, we have explored every facet of this journey, from the initial considerations of why to start a hardware store and whether it's the right fit for you, to the intricate details of market research, legal considerations, financing, store design, staffing, marketing, operations, and various expansion strategies.

The hardware store industry is a dynamic and competitive one, marked by changing consumer preferences, evolving technologies, and shifting market trends. To thrive in this environment, you must be adaptable, customer-focused, and committed to delivering a top-notch shopping experience.

Key takeaways from this guide include:

Understanding Your Market: Thorough market research is the foundation of your hardware store's success. Knowing your target audience, competition, and location dynamics will guide your business decisions.

Legal and Regulatory Compliance: Navigating the legal and regulatory landscape is crucial. Choosing the right business structure, obtaining permits, and ensuring health and safety compliance are non-negotiable steps.

Financing and Budgeting: Carefully estimate your startup costs, secure funding, and manage your finances diligently. Budgeting and financial planning are essential for long-term sustainability.

Store Design and Layout: A well-designed store layout, effective shelving, and attractive merchandising contribute to a pleasant shopping experience that keeps customers coming back.

Product Selection and Suppliers: Building strong relationships with suppliers, managing inventory efficiently, setting competitive prices, and exploring private label options are key to product selection and procurement.

Staffing and Management: Hiring and training a motivated team, establishing employee policies, efficient scheduling, and performance evaluation are essential for smooth store operations.

Marketing and Promotion: Developing a comprehensive marketing plan, building a strong brand image, implementing effective advertising strategies, and utilizing loyalty programs are vital for attracting and retaining customers.

Operations and Logistics: Managing daily store operations, optimizing supply chain management, controlling inventory, and maintaining quality assurance are the cornerstones of a well-run hardware store.

Growth and Expansion: Strategies such as expanding your product line, opening additional locations, exploring franchising opportunities, and venturing into international markets offer avenues for growth and expansion.

In the hardware store business, customer satisfaction is paramount. By providing a wide variety of quality products, exceptional service, and a seamless shopping experience, you can build a loyal customer base and position your store for long-term success.

Remember that success in the hardware industry requires ongoing adaptability, a commitment to innovation, and a dedication to maintaining the highest standards of quality and customer service. As you embark on this journey, may this guide serve as a valuable resource to help you navigate the challenges and seize the opportunities that come your way in the world of hardware retail. Best of luck on your path to building a thriving hardware store business.

www.ingramcontent.com/pod-product-compliance
Lightning Source LLC
Chambersburg PA
CBHW062350290526
45794CB00005B/2169